This insert, which contains revised music, serves to replace pages 10,11, and 12 of

Alvin Singleton's *Argoru V/a.*

multiphonic

molto meno mosso

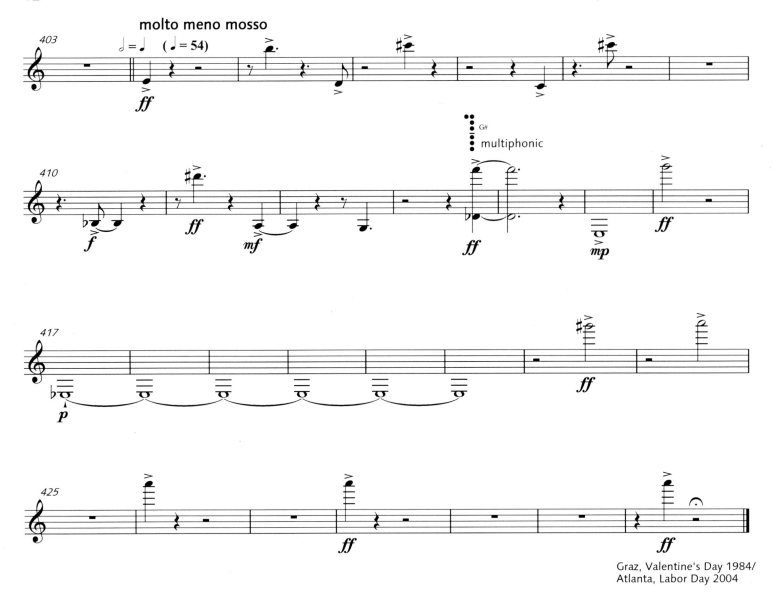

multiphonic

G#

Graz, Valentine's Day 1984/
Atlanta, Labor Day 2004

Edition Schott

Alvin Singleton

b. 1940

Argoru V/a

for bass clarinet

ED 30005
ISMN M-60001-051-6

www.schott-music.com

Mainz · London · Madrid · New York · Paris · Prague · Tokyo · Toronto
© 2009 SCHOTT MUSIC CORPORATION · Printed in the USA

Foreword

Argoru V/a is a unique work for solo bass clarinet that blends Singleton's superb sequential treatment of material and clarity of form in a contemporary jazz setting. From the "Blues-like" introduction to the "swing" sections, phrasing and detailed articulation markings reflect the author's close ties to the jazz idiom. His successful incorporation of extended techniques for the instrument, such as slap tongue and multiphonics, make this piece a very attractive addition to the solo bass clarinet repertoire.

—David Keberle

The original version of ARGORU V/a was composed for Harry Sparnaay and premiered on March 8, 1984 at IRCAM-Centre Georges Pompidou in Paris, France.

The notation 𝅘𝅥 means slap tongue.

Edited by David Keberle

4

for Harry Sparnaay

ARGORU V/a

Alvin Singleton (1984/rev. 2004)

ff tutta la forza

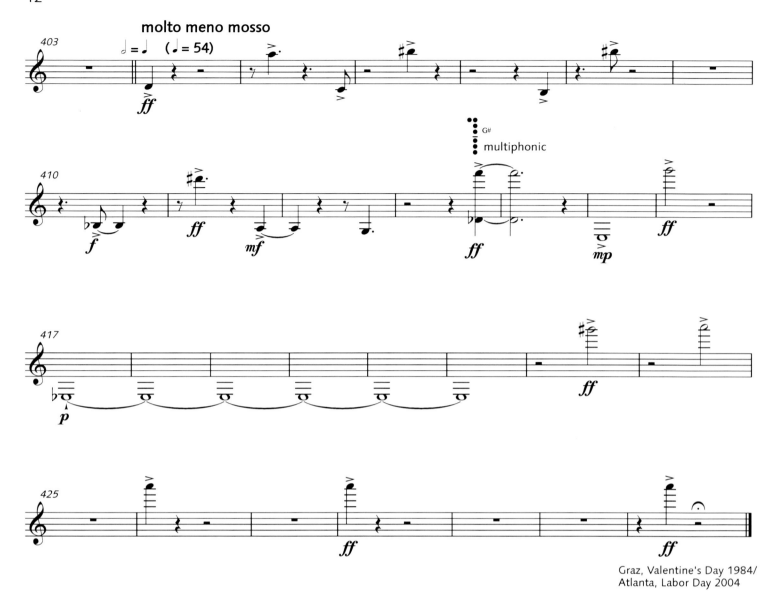

Graz, Valentine's Day 1984/
Atlanta, Labor Day 2004